548-5798

Please Return to

Love Letters

Love
Letters

Love Letters

by

A.R. Gurney

The Fireside Theatre

Garden City, NY

SPECIAL NOTE

Photographs by Anita and Steve Shevett
Manufactured in the United States of America

Quality Printing and Binding by:
BERRYVILLE GRAPHICS
P.O. Box 272
Berryville, VA 22611 U.S.A.

LOVE LETTERS was initially presented by the Long Wharf Theater (Arvin Brown, Artistic Director; M. Edgar Rosenblum, Executive Director) in New Haven, Connecticut, on November 3, 1988. It was directed by John Tillinger; the lighting was by Judy Rasmuson; and the production stage manager was Beverly J. Andreozzi. The cast was as follows:

ANDREW MAKEPEACE LADD III . . . . . John Rubinstein
MELISSA GARDNER . . . . Joanna Gleason

LOVE LETTERS was subsequently presented by Roger L. Stevens, Thomas Viertel, Steven Baruch and Richard Frankel at the Promenade Theatre (under the direction of Ben Sprecher and William P. Miller) in New York City on February 13, 1989. It was directed by John Tillinger; the lighting was by Dennis Parichy; casting was by Linda Wright; and the production stage manager was William H. Lang. The cast was as follows:

ANDREW MAKEPEACE LADD III . . . . . John Rubinstein
MELISSA GARDNER . . . . Kathleen Turner

LOVE LETTERS opened on Broadway at the Edison Theatre on October 31, 1989. The cast was as follows:

ANDREW MAKEPEACE LADD III . . . . . . Jason Robards
MELISSA GARDNER . . . . Colleen Dewhurst

AUTHOR'S NOTE

This is a play, or rather a sort of a play, which needs no theatre, no lengthy rehearsal, no special set, no memorization of lines, and no commitment from its two actors beyond the night of performance. It is designed simply to be read aloud by an actor and an actress of roughly the same age, sitting side by side at a table, in front of a group of people of any size. The actor might wear a dark gray suit, the actress a simple, expensive-looking dress. In a more formal production, the table and chairs might be reasonably elegant English antiques, and the actors' area may be isolated against a dark background by bright, focused lights. In performance, the piece would seem to work best if the actors didn't look at each other until the end, when Melissa might watch Andy as he reads his final letter. They *listen* eagerly and actively to each other along the way, however, much as we might listen to an urgent voice on a one-way radio, coming from far, far away.

To my wife

Love Letters

PART ONE

ANDY

Andrew Makepeace Ladd, the Third, accepts with pleasure the kind invitation of Mr. and Mrs. Gilbert Channing Gardner for a birthday party in honor of their daughter Melissa on April 19th, 1937, at half past three o'clock . . .

MELISSA

Dear Andy: Thank you for the birthday present. I have a lot of Oz books, but not *The Lost Princess of Oz*. What made you give me that one? Sincerely yours, Melissa.

ANDY

I'm answering your letter about the book. When you came into second grade with that stuck-up nurse, you looked like a lost princess.

MELISSA

I don't believe what you wrote. I think my mother told your mother to get that book. I like the pictures more than the words. Now let's stop writing letters.

* * *

1

ANDY

I will make my l's taller than my d's.

MELISSA

I will close up my a's and my o's.

ANDY

I will try to make longer p's. Pass it on.

MELISSA

You're funny.

* * *

ANDY

Will you be my valentine?

MELISSA

Were you the one who sent me a valentine saying "Will you be my valentine?"

ANDY

Yes I sent it.

MELISSA

Then I will be. Unless I have to kiss you.

* * *

ANDY

When it's warmer out, can I come over and swim in your pool?

MELISSA

No you can't. I have a new nurse named Miss Hawthorne who thinks you'll give me infantile paralysis.

ANDY

Will you help me go down and get milk and cookies during recess?

MELISSA

I will if you don't ask me to marry you again.

BOTH

I will not write personal notes in class, I will not write personal notes in class, I will not . . .

* * *

ANDY

Merry Christmas and Happy New Year. Love, Andy Ladd.

MELISSA

I made this card myself. It's not Santa Claus. It's a kangaroo jumping over a glass of orange juice. Do you like it? I like YOU. Melissa.

3

ANDY

My mother says I have to apologize in writing. I apologize for sneaking into the girls' bath-house while you were changing into your bathing suit. Tell Miss Hawthorne I apologize to her, too.

MELISSA

Here is a picture of you and me without our bathing suits on. Guess which one is you. Don't show this to ANYONE. I love you.

ANDY

Here is a picture of Miss Hawthorne without her bathing suit on.

MELISSA

You can't draw very well, can you?

* * *

ANDY

Thank you for sending me the cactus plant stuck in the little donkey. I've gotten lots of presents here in the hospital and I have to write thank-you notes for every one. I hate it here. My throat is sore all the time from where they cut out my tonsils. They give me lots of ice cream, but they also take my temperature the wrong way.

* * *

4

MELISSA

Merry Christmas and Happy New Year. Why did they send you to another school this year?

ANDY

Merry Christmas. They think I should be with all boys.

* * *

MELISSA

You made me promise to send you a postcard. This is it.

ANDY

You're supposed to write personal notes on the backs of postcards. For example, here are some questions to help you think of things to say. Do you like Lake Saranac? Is it fun visiting your grandmother? Are your parents really getting divorced? Can you swim out into the deep part of that lake, or does Miss Hawthorne make you stay in the shallow part where it's all roped off? Is there anybody there my age? I mean boys. Please write answers to all these questions.

MELISSA

No. No. Yes. Yes. No.

* * *

ANDY

Dear Melissa. Remember me? Andy Ladd? They've sent me to camp so I can be with all boys again. This is quiet hour so we have to write home, but I've already done that, so I'm writing you. There's a real Indian here named Iron Crow who takes us on Nature walks and teaches us six new plants a day. This is O.K., except he forgot about poison ivy. I won the backstroke, which gives me two and a half gold stars. If I get over fifty gold stars by Parent's Day, then I win a Leadership Prize which is what my father expects of me. I'm making a napkin-ring in shop which is worth four stars and which is either for my mother or for you. I hope you'll write me back, because when the mail comes every morning, they shout out our names and it would be neat to walk up and get a letter from a girl.

MELISSA

Help! Eeeek! Yipes! I can't write LETTERS! It took me HOURS just to write "Dear Andy." I write my father because I miss him so much, but to write a BOY! Hell's Bells and Oriental Smells! I'm sending you this picture I drew of our cat instead. Don't you love his expression? It's not quite right, but I tried three times. I drew those jiggly lines around his tail because sometimes the tail behaves like a completely separate person. I love that tail. There's a part of me that feels like that tail. Oh, and here's some bad news. My mother's gotten married again to a man named Hooper McPhail. HELP! LEMME OUTA HERE!

6

ANDY

I liked the cat. Is that the cat you threw in the pool that time when we were playing over at your house in third grade?

MELISSA

No, that was a different cat entirely.

* * *

ANDY

This is a dumb Halloween card and wouldn't scare anyone, but I'm really writing about dancing school. My parents say I have to go this year, but I don't see why I have to. I can't figure out why they keep sending us away from girls and then telling us we have to be with them. Are you going to dancing school also? Just write Yes or No, since you hate writing.

MELISSA

Yes. *flatly*

* * *

ANDY

Dear Mrs. McPhail. I want to apologize to you for my behavior in the back of your car coming home last night from dancing school. Charlie and I were just goofing around and I guess it just got out of

7

hand. I'm sorry you had to pull over to the curb and I'm sorry we tore Melissa's dress. My father says you should send me the bill and I'll pay for it out of my allowance.

MELISSA

Dear Andy. Mummy brought your letter up here to Lake Placid. She thought it was cute. I thought it was dumb. I could tell your father made you write it. You and I both know that the fight in the car was really Charlie's fault. And Charlie never apologized, thank God. That's why I like him, actually. As for you, you shouldn't always do what your parents WANT, Andy. Even at dancing school you're always doing just the RIGHT THING all the time. You're a victim of your parents sometimes. That was why I picked Charlie to do the rumba with me that time. He at least hacks around occasionally. I'm enclosing a picture I drew of a dancing bear on a chain. That's you, Andy. Sometimes. I swear.

ANDY

I know it seems jerky, but I like writing, actually. I like writing compositions in English, I like writing letters, I like writing you. I wanted to write that letter to your mother because I knew you'd see it, so it was like talking to you when you weren't here. And when you couldn't *interrupt*. (Hint, hint.) My father says everyone should write letters as much as they can. It's a dying art. He says letters are a way of presenting yourself in the best possible light to another person. I think that, too.

MELISSA

I think you sound too much like your father. But I'm not going to argue by MAIL and anyway the skiing's too good.

ANDY

Get well soon. I'm sorry you broke your leg.

MELISSA

Mummy says I broke it purposely because I'm a self-destructive person and went down Whiteface Mountain without asking permission. All I know is I wish I had broken my arm instead so I'd have a good excuse not to write LETTERS. I'm enclosing a picture I drew of the bed pan. I'm SERIOUS! Don't you love its shape?

* * *

ANDY

Andrew M. Ladd, III, accepts with pleasure the kind invitation of Mrs. R. Ferguson Brown for a dinner in honor of her granddaughter Melissa Gardner before the Children's Charity Ball.

angry MELISSA

I'm writing this letter because I'm scared if I called you up, I'd start crying, right on the telephone. I'm really MAD at you, Andy. Don't you know that when you're invited to a dinner before a dance,

9

you're supposed to dance with the person giving it at least TWICE. (And I don't mean my grand-mother either.) That's why they *give* dinner par-ties. So people get *danced* with. I notice you danced with Ginny Waters, but you never danced with me once. (I just think it's rude, that's all.) Straighten up and fly right, Andy. How do you expect to get anywhere in life if you're rude to women? Nuts to you, Andy, and that goes double on Sunday!

ANDY

I didn't dance with you because I've got a stretched groin. If you don't know what that means, look it up some time. I was going to tell you in person but I got embarrassed. I stretched it playing hockey last week. The only reason I danced with Ginny Waters is she takes tiny steps, but you always make me do those big spins and we could have gotten into serious trouble. I tried it out at home with my mother first, and it hurt like hell. That's why I didn't dance with you. I'm using a heating pad now and maybe we can dance next week at the junior assemblies.

MELISSA

I don't believe that hockey stuff. I think Ginny Waters stretched your groin. And next time you cut in, I'm going to stretch the other one.

ANDY

Huh? You obviously don't know what a groin in.

MELISSA

You obviously don't know what a joke is.

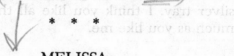

* * *

MELISSA

Merry Christmas and Happy New Year. Guess what? I'm going to a psychiatrist now. My mother says it will do me a world of good. Don't tell anyone, though. It's supposed to be a big secret.

ANDY

Merry Christmas and Happy New Year. I have a question and would you please write the answer *by mail,* because sometimes when you call, my mother listens on the telephone, and when she doesn't my little brother does. Here's the question: do you talk about sex with the psychiatrist?

MELISSA

I talk about sex all the time. It's terribly expensive, but I think it's worth it.

ANDY

If I went to a psychiatrist, I'd talk about you. Seriously. I would. I think about you quite often.

11

MELISSA

Sometimes I think you like me because I'm richer than you are. Sometimes I really have that feeling. I think you like the pool, and the elevator in my grandmother's house, and Simpson in his butler's coat coming in with gingerale and cookies on a silver tray. I think you like all that stuff just as much as you like me.

ANDY

All I know is my mother keeps saying you'd make a good match. She says if I ever married you, I'd be set up for life. But I think it's really just physical attraction. That's why I liked going into the elevator with you at your grandmother's that time. Want to try it again?

* * *

MELISSA

HELP! LEMME OUTA HERE! They shipped me off to this nunnery! It's the end of the absolute WORLD! We have to wear these sappy middy-blouses, and learn POSTURE in gym, and speak French out LOUD in class. "Aide-moi, mon cheva-lier!" Oh God, it's crappy here. All the girls squeal and shriek, and you can hear them barfing in the bathroom after the evening meal. We can only go to Hartford one day a week IF we can find a chap-erone, and there are only two dances with boys a year, and if we're caught drinking, even *beer*, it's

12

wham, bam, onto the next train home, which is WORSE! Can you come visit me some Sunday afternoon? We can invite boys to tea from four to six. There are all these biddies sitting around keeping watch, but if the weather's good, we could walk up and down the driveway before we have to sign in for evening prayers. They've made me room with this fat, spoiled Cuban bitch who has nine pairs of shoes, and all she does is lie on her bed and listen to *Finian's Rainbow.* "How are Things in Glocca Morra?" Who gives a shit how things are *there?* It's here where they're miserable. The walls of this cell are puke-green, and you can't pin anything up except school banners and pictures of your stupid family. What family? Am I supposed to sit and look at a picture of Hooper McPhail? Come save me, Andy. Or at least WRITE! Just so I hear a boy's voice, even on paper.

ANDY

Just got your letter. They shipped me off too. Last-minute decision. Your mother told my mother it would do me good. She said I was a diamond in the rough. I'll write as soon as I'm smoother.

MELISSA

Dear Diamond. You, too? Oh, I give up. Why do they keep pushing us together and then pulling us apart? I think we're all being brought up by a bunch of foolish farts. Now we'll *have* to write letters which I hate. But don't let them smooth you out, Andy. I like the rough parts. In fact, some-

13

times I think you ought to be a little rougher. Love.
Me.

ANDY

I'm very sorry to be so late in replying but I
haven't had much time. I also have a lot of obligations. I have to write my parents once a week, and
three out of four grandparents, *separately,* once a
month, and Minnie, our cook, who sent me a box of
fudge. Plus I have all my schoolwork to do, includ-
ing a composition once a week for English and
another for history. My grandmother gave me a
new Parker 51 and some writing paper with my
name on it as a going-away present, but still, that's
a lot of writing I have to do. Last week I was so tied
up I skipped my weekly letter to my parents, and
my father called the school long-distance about it.
I had to go up on the carpet in front of the Rector
and say I wasn't sick or anything, I was just working, and so I had to write my parents three pages to
make up for the week I missed. So that's why I
haven't written till now. (Whew!) School is going
well, I guess. In English, we're now finishing up
Milton's *Paradise Lost.* In history, we're studying
the causes and results of the Thirty Years War. I
think the Catholics caused it. In Latin, we're trans-
lating Cicero's orations against Catiline. "How
long, O Catiline, will you abuse our patience?"
When I get home, I'm going to try that on my little
brother. In French, we have to sit and listen to Mr.
Thatcher read out loud all the parts in *Androma-
che,* by Jean Racine. It's supposed to be a great
masterpiece, but the class comes right after foot-

14

ball practice, so it's a little hard to stay awake. In Sacred Studies, we have to compare and contrast all four gospels. It's hard to believe they're all talking about the same guy. In Math, we're trying to factor with two unknowns. Sometimes I let X be me and Y be you, and you'd be amazed how it comes out.

My grades are pretty good. They post your weekly average outside study hall and last week I got 91.7 overall average. Not bad, eh? I got a letter from my grandfather telling me not to be first in my class because only the Jews are first. I wrote him and told him I wasn't first, but even if I was, there are no Jews here. We have a few Catholics, but they're not too smart, actually. I don't think you can be smart and Catholic at the same time.

I was elected to the Student Council and I'm arguing for three things: one, I think we should have outside sports, rather than keeping them all intramural. I think it would be better to play with Exeter than just play with ourselves. Two, I think we should have more than one dance a year. I think female companionship can be healthy occasionally, even for younger boys. And three, I think we should only have to go to chapel *once* on Sunday. I think it's important to pray to be a better guy, and all that, but if you have to do it all day long, you can get quite boring. And if you get boring to yourself, think how boring you must be to God.

I'm playing left tackle on the third team, and I'll be playing hockey, *of course,* this winter, and I think I'll try rowing this spring since I always stank at baseball.

15

Now I have to memorize the last five lines of *Paradise Lost*. Hold it . . . Back in a little while . . . There. That wasn't so hard, maybe because it reminds me of you and me, sent away from home. I'll write it down for you:

Some natural tears they dropp'd, but wip'd
them soon;
The World was all before them, where to choose
Their place of rest, and providence their guide:
They hand in hand with wand'ring steps and
slow,
Through Eden took their solitary way.

There you are. I wrote that without looking at the book, and it's right, too, because I just checked it, word by word. It's not so bad, is it? In fact, it sounds great if you recite it in the bathroom, when no one is in the shower or taking a dump. Love, Andy.

MELISSA

Thanks for your letter which was a little too long. I guess you have a lot of interesting things to say, Andy, but some of them are not terribly interesting to me. I want to hear more about your FEEL-INGS. For instance, here are MY feelings. This place STINKS, but I don't want to go back home because Hooper McPhail stinks, and I haven't heard of another boarding school that DOESN'T stink, which means that LIFE stinks in general. Those are my feelings for this week. Write soon. Love, me.

ANDY

One feeling I have almost all the time is that I miss
my dog, Porgy. Remember him? Our black cocker
who peed in the vestibule when you patted him
when you came back to our house after the skating
party. I miss him all the time. Some of the masters
up here have dogs, and when I pat them I miss
Porgy even more. I dream about him. I wrote a
composition about him for English called "Will He
Remember?" and got a 96 on it. It was about how I
remember him, but will he remember me? I have
a picture of him on my bureau right next to my
parents. By the way, could I have your picture,
too?

MELISSA

Here's a picture of me taken at the Hartford bus
station. I was all set to run away and then decided
not to. This is all you get until I get my braces off
Christmas vacation. Don't look at my hair. I'm
changing it. By the way, do you know a boy there
named Spencer Willis? There's a girl here, Annie
Abbott, who met him in Edgartown last summer
and thinks he's cute. Would you ask him what he
thinks of her?

ANDY

Spencer Willis says Annie Abbott is a potential
nympho. I'm sorry to tell you this, but it's true.

17

MELISSA

Annie says to tell Spencer he's a total turkey. Tell him she'd write and say so herself but she's scared of barfing all over the page.

ANDY

Do you get out for Thanksgiving? We don't, because of the war.

MELISSA

We do, but I don't. I've been grounded just for smoking one lousy Chesterfield out behind the art studio. So now I have to stay here and eat stale turkey with Cubans and Californians. That's all right. I was supposed to meet Mummy in New York, but it looks like she can't be there anyway because she's going to Reno to divorce Hooper McPhail. Yippee! Yay! He was a jerk and a pill, and he used to bother me in bed, if you must know.

* * *

ANDY

I liked seeing you Christmas vacation, particularly with your braces off. I really liked necking with you in the Watsons' rumpus room. Will you go steady with me?

MELISSA

I don't believe in going steady. It's against my religion. I hated that stuff with all those pairs of pim-

18

ply people in the Watsons' basement, leaning on each other, swaying to that dumb music with all the lights off. If that's going steady, I say screw it. My mother says you should meet as many boys as you can before you have to settle down and marry one of them. That way you'll make less of a mistake. It didn't work for her but maybe it will work for me.

ANDY

Can we at least go to the movies together during spring vacation?

MELISSA

I don't know, Andy. I like seeing you, but I don't want to go home much any more. My mother gets drunk a lot, if you must know, and comes into my room all the time, and talks endlessly about I don't know what because she slurs her words. The only really good time I had was when I came over to your house Christmas Eve. That was fun. Singing around the piano, hanging up the stockings, playing Chinese Checkers with your brother, helping your mother with the gravy. I liked all that. You may not have as much money as we have, but you've got a better family. So spring vacation I'm going to visit my grandmother in Palm Beach. Ho hum. At least I'll get a tan. P.S. Enclosed is a picture I drew of your dog Porgy who I remember from Christmas Eve. The nose is wrong, but don't you think the eyes are good?

ANDY

I'm stroking the 4th crew now. Yesterday, I rowed number 2 on the 3rd. Tomorrow I may row number 6 on the 2nd or number 4 on the 5th. Who knows? You get out there and work your butt off, and the launch comes alongside and looks you over, and the next day they post a list on the bulletin board saying who will row what. They never tell you what you did right or wrong, whether you're shooting your slide or bending your back or what. They just post the latest results for all to see. Some days I think I'm doing really well, and I get sent down two crews. One day I was obviously hacking around, and they moved me UP. There's no rhyme or reason. I went to Mr. Clark who is the head of rowing and I said, "Look, Mr. Clark. There's something wrong about this system. People are constantly moving up and down and no one knows why. It doesn't seem to have anything to do with whether you're good or bad, strong or weak, coordinated or uncoordinated. It all seems random, *sir.*" And Mr. Clark said, "That's life, Andy." And walked away. Well maybe that's life, but it doesn't *have* to be life. You could easily make rules which made sense, so the good ones moved up and the bad ones moved down, and people *knew* what was going on. I'm serious. I'm thinking about going to law school later on.

MELISSA

Your last letter was too much about rowing. Do you know a boy there named Steve Scully. I met him

20

down in Florida, and he said he went to your
school, and was on the first crew. He said he was
the fastest rower in the boat. Is that true, or was he
lying? I think he may have been lying.

ANDY

Steve Scully was lying. He doesn't even row. And if
he did, and rowed faster than everyone else in the
same boat, he'd mess the whole thing up. He said
he got to second base with you. Is that true?

MELISSA

Steve Scully is a lying son of a bitch, and you can
tell him I said so.

* * *

ANDY

Will you be around this summer? I think I've got a
summer job caddying, so no more camp, Thank
God.

MELISSA

I'll be visiting my father in California. I haven't
seen him in four years. He has a new wife, and I
have two half-sisters now. It's like going to find a
whole new family. Oh I hope, I hope . . .

ANDY

Do you like California?

21

Write me about California. How's your second
family?

Did you get my letters? I checked with your
mother, and I had the correct address. How come
you haven't answered me all summer?

Back at school now. Hope everything's O.K. with
you. Did you get my letters out in California, or did
you have a wicked step-mother who confiscated
them?

MELISSA

I don't want to talk about California. Ever. For a
while I thought I had two families, but now I know
I really don't have any. You're very lucky, Andy.
You don't know it, but you are. But maybe I'm
lucky, too. In another way. I was talking to Mrs.
Wadsworth who comes in from Hartford to teach
us art. She says I have a real talent both in drawing
and in painting, and she's going to try me out in
pottery as well. She says some afternoon she's going to take me just by myself to her studio in Hartford, and we'll do life drawings of her lover in just a
jock-strap! Don't laugh. She says art and sex are
sort of the same thing.

ANDY

Dear Melissa. I have four questions, so please concentrate. One: will you come up to the mid-winter dance? Two, If so, can you arrive on the eleven-twenty-two Friday night train? Three, Does the Rector's wife have to write your Headmistress telling her where you will be staying? Four. Does the Rector's wife also have to write your mother?

MELISSA

The answer is yes, except for my mother, who won't care.

* * *

ANDY

I have to tell you this, right off the bat. I'm really goddam mad at you. I invite you up here for the only dance my class has been able to go to since we got here, I meet you at the train and buy you a vanilla milkshake and bring you out to school in a taxi, I score two goals for you during the hockey game the next afternoon, I buy you the eight dollar gardenia corsage, I make sure your dance card is filled with the most regular guys in the school, and then what happens? I now hear that you sneaked off with Bob Bartram during the Vienna Waltz, and necked with him in the coatroom. I heard that from two guys! And then Bob himself brought it up yesterday at breakfast. He says he French-kissed you and touched BOTH your breasts. I tried to punch him but Mr. Enbody restrained me. I'm really sore, Melissa. I consider this a betrayal of everything I hold near and dear. Particularly since you would hardly even let me kiss you goodnight after we had cocoa at the Rector's. And you know what I'm talking about, too! So don't expect any more letters from me, or any telephone calls either during spring vacation. Sincerely yours.

MELISSA

Sorry, sorry, sorry. I AM! I HATE that Bob Bartram. I hated him even when I necked with him. I know you won't believe that, but it's true. You can be attracted to someone you hate. Well, maybe *you* can't, but I can. So all right, I necked with him, but he never touched my chest, and if he says he did, he should be strung up by his testicles. You tell him that, for me, at breakfast! Anyway, I got carried away, Andy, and I'm a stupid bitch, and I'm sorry. I felt so guilty about it that I didn't want to kiss you after the cocoa.

And besides, Andy. Gulp. Er. Ah. Um. How do I say this? With you it's different. You're like a friend to me. You're like a brother. I've never had a brother, and I don't have too many friends, so you're both, Andy. You're it. My mother says you must never say that to a man, but I'm saying it anyway and it's true. Maybe if I didn't know you so well, maybe if I hadn't grown up with you, maybe if we hadn't written all these goddamn LETTERS

24

all the time, I could have kissed you the way I kissed Bob Bartram.

Oh, but PLEASE let's see each other spring vacation. Please. I count on you, Andy. I NEED you. I think sometimes I'd go stark raving mad if I didn't have you to hold onto. I really think that sometimes. Much love.

* * *

Happy Easter! I know no one sends Easter cards except maids, but here's mine anyway, drawn with my own hot little hands. I drew those tears on that corny bunny on the left because it misses you so much, but maybe I've just made it all the cornier.

* * *

Greetings from Palm Beach. Decided to visit my grandmother. Yawn, yawn. I'm a whiz at backgammon and gin-rummy. Hear you took Gretchen Lascelles to see *Quo Vadis* and sat in the *loges* and put your arm around her and smoked! Naughty, naughty!

* * *

Back at school, but not for long, that's for sure. Caught nipping gin in the woods with Bubbles Harriman. Have to pack my trunk by tonight and be out tomorrow. Mummy's frantically pulling strings all over the Eastern Seaboard for another school. Mrs. Wadsworth, my art teacher, thinks I should chuck it all and go to Italy and study art.

25

What do you think? Oh, please write, Andy,
PLEASE. I need your advice, or are you too busy
thinking about Gretchen Lascelles?

* * *

ANDY

To answer your question about Italy, I think you're
too young to go. My Mother said she had a room-
mate once who went to Italy in the summer, and
the Italians pinched her all the time on the rear
end. Mother says she became thoroughly over-
stimulated. So I think you should go to another
school, graduate, go to college, and maybe after
that, when you're more *mature*, you could go to
Italy. That's my advice, for what it's worth, which
is probably not much, the way things are going
between you and me.

* * *

MELISSA

Here I am at Emma Willard's Academy for Young
Lesbians. Help! Lemme outa here! "Plus ca
change, plus c'est le same shit." Are you coming
straight home this June because I am. I want to see
you. Or are you still in love with Gretchen Lascelles?

ANDY

For your information, I'm not taking Gretchen
Lascelles out any more. I brought her home after

26

the Penneys' party, and my father caught us on the couch. He told me that he didn't care what kind of girls I took out, as long as I didn't bring them around my mother. Even though my mother was up in bed. Still, I guess Gretchen can be embarrassing to older people.

MELISSA

I hope to see you in June, then.

ANDY

Can't come home in June. Sorry. I have to go and be a counselor at the school camp for poor kids from the urban slums. I'm Vice President of my class now, and I'm supposed to set an example of social responsibility all through July. I'll be writing you letters, though, and I hope you'll write me.

MELISSA

I don't want to write letters all the time. I really don't. I want to see you.

ANDY

You just need more confidence in your letter-writing ability. Sometimes you manage to attain a very vivid style.

MELISSA

Won't you please just stop writing about writing, and come home and go to the Campbells' sports

27

party before you go up to that stupid camp? PLEASE! I behave better when you're around. In PERSON! PLEASE!

* * *

ANDY

Greetings from New Hampshire. This card shows the town we're near, where we sneak in and buy beer. We're cleaning the place up now, and putting out the boat docks, and caulking the canoes, because the kids arrive tomorrow. Gotta go. Write soon.

MELISSA

I miss you. I really wish you had come to the Campbells' sports party.

ANDY

Dear Melissa. Sandy McCarthy arrived from home for the second shift here at camp, and he told me all about the Campbells' sports party. He said you wore a two piece bathing suit and ran around goosing girls and pushing boys into the pool. Do you enjoy that sort of crap? He said the other girls were furious at you. Don't you want the respect of other women? Sandy also said you let Bucky Zeller put a tennis ball into your cleavage. Are you a nympho or what? Don't you ever just like sitting down somewhere and making conversation? Sandy says you're turning into a hot box. Do you like having

that reputation? Hell, I thought there was a differ-
ence between you and Gretchen Lascelles. Maybe
I was wrong. Don't you care about anything in this
world except hacking around? Don't you feel any
obligation to help the poor people, for example?
Sometimes I think your big problem is you're so
rich you don't have enough to do, and so you start
playing grab-ass with people. I'm sorry to say these
things, but what Sandy told me made me slightly
disgusted, frankly.

* * *

I wrote you a letter from New Hampshire. Did you
receive it?

* * *

Are you there, or are you visiting your grandmother, or what?

* * *

Are you sore at me? I'll bet you're sore at me.

* * *

I'm sorry. I apologize. I'm a stuffy bastard sometimes, aren't I?

* * *

The hell with you, then.

29

MELISSA

Oooh. Big, tough Andy using four-letter words like hell.

ANDY

Screw you!

MELISSA

Don't you wish you could!

ANDY

Everyone else seems to be.

MELISSA

Don't believe everything you read in the papers.

* * *

Dear Andrew Makepeace Ladd, the Turd: I just want you to know you hurt me very much. I just want you to know that. Now let's just leave each other ALONE for a while. All right? All right.

* * *

ANDY

Dear Melissa: My mother wrote me that your grandmother had died. Please accept my deepest sympathies.

30

MELISSA

Thank you for your note about my grandmother. I loved her a lot even though she could be a little boring.

ANDY

Congratulations on getting into Briarcliff. I hear it's great.

MELISSA

Thank you for your note about Briarcliff. It's not great and you know it. In fact, it's a total pit. But it's close to New York and I can take the train in and take drawing at the Institute three days a week. And in two years, if I stick it out, Mummy's promised that I can go live in Florence. I hope you like Yale.

ANDY

Would you consider coming to the Yale-Dartmouth game, Saturday, Oct 28th?

MELISSA

I'll be there.

ANDY

Uh-oh. Damn! I'm sorry, Melissa. I have to cancel. My parents have decided to visit that weekend, and they come first, according to them. My mother

31

says she'd love to have you with us, but my father thinks you can be somewhat distracting.

MELISSA

You and your parents. Let me know when you decide to grow up.

ANDY

How about the Harvard game, November 16th?

MELISSA

Do you plan to grow up at the Harvard game?

ANDY

Give me a chance. I might surprise you.

MELISSA

O.K. Let's give it a try. You should know that I'm even richer now than when you said I was rich, thanks to poor Granny. I plan to drive up to the front gate of Calhoun College in my new red Chrysler convertible, and sit there stark naked, honking my horn and drinking champagne and flashing at all the Freshmen.

ANDY

Here's the schedule. We'll have lunch at Calhoun around noon. Then drive out to the game. Then there's a Sea-Breeze party at the Fence Club after-

32

wards, and an Egg Nog brunch at Saint Anthony's the next day. I'll reserve a room for you at the Taft or the Duncan, probably the Taft, since the Duncan is a pretty seedy joint.

MELISSA

Make it the Duncan. I hear the Taft is loaded with parents, all milling around the lobby, keeping tabs on who goes up in the elevators. Can't WAIT till the 16th.

ANDY

The Duncan it is. Hubba hubba, Goodyear rubba!

* * *

MELISSA

Dear Andy. This is supposed to be a thank-you note for the Yale-Harvard weekend, but I don't feel like writing one, and I think you know why. Love, Melissa.

ANDY

Dear Melissa. I keep thinking about the weekend. I can't get it out of my mind. It wasn't much good, was it? I don't mean just the Duncan, I mean the whole thing. We didn't really click, did we? I always had the sense that you were looking over my shoulder, looking for someone else, and ditto with me. Both of us seemed to be expecting something different from what was there.

33

As for the Hotel Duncan, I don't know. Maybe I had too many Sea-Breezes. Maybe you did. But what I really think is that there were too many people in that hotel room. Besides you and me, it seemed my mother was there, egging us on, and my father shaking his head, and *your* mother zonked out on the couch, and Miss Hawthorne and your *grand*mother, sitting on the sidelines, watching us like hawks. Anyway, I was a dud. I admit it. I'm sorry. I went to the Infirmary on Monday and talked to the Doctor about it, and he said these things happen all the time. Particularly when there's a lot of pressure involved. The woman doesn't have to worry about it so much, but the man does. Anyway, it didn't happen with Gretchen Lascelles. You can write her and ask her if you want.

MELISSA

You know what I think is wrong? These letters. These goddamn letters. That's what's wrong with us, in my humble opinion. I know you more from your LETTERS than I do in person. Maybe that's why I was looking over your shoulder. I was looking for the person who's been in these letters all these years. Or for the person who's NOT in these letters. I don't know. All I know is you're not quite the same when I see you, Andy. You're really not. I'm not saying you're a jerk in person. I'm not saying that at all. I'm just saying that all this letter-writing has messed us up. It's a bad habit. It's made us seem like people we're not. So maybe what was wrong was that there were two people *missing* in the Hotel Duncan that night: namely, the real you and the real me.

ANDY

Whatever the matter is, we're in real trouble, you and I. That I realize. So now, what do we do about it? Maybe we should just concentrate on dancing together. Then we can still hold each other and move together and get very subtly sexy with each other, and not have to deliver the goods all the time, if you know what I mean. Come to think of it, maybe that's why they sent us to dancing school in the first place. Maybe that's why dancing was invented.

MELISSA

At least we should stop writing LETTERS for a while. You could start telephoning me, actually. Here is our dorm number: WILSON 1-2486.

ANDY

I hate talking to you on the telephone. Yours is in the hall and ours is right by the college dining room. People are always coming and going and making cracks. Telephoning is not letter-writing at all.

MELISSA

I called the telephone company and they've put a private phone in my room. ROGERS 2-2403. It's sort of expensive, but at least we can TALK!

35

ANDY

The reason I'm writing is because your phone's always busy. Or else ours is. And I can't afford a private one. Maybe we should just start writing letters again.

MELISSA

No letters! Please! Now order that telephone! I'll lend you the dough. Just think about it. You can talk back and forth, and hear someone's real voice, and get to know someone in LIFE, rather than on WRITING PAPER, for God's sake! Now get that phone! Please!

* * *

ANDY

I'm writing because when I telephoned, you just hung up on me. One thing about letters: you can't hang up on them.

MELISSA

You can tear up letters, though. Enclosed are the pieces. Send them to Angela Atkinson at Sarah Lawrence.

ANDY

What the hell is the matter?

36

ANDREW: I love to write. . . . I love writing you. . . . I feel like a true lover when I'm writing you. This letter, which I'm writing with my own hand . . . comes from me and no one else, and is a present of myself to you. . . . You can tear me up and throw me out, or keep me, and read me today, tomorrow, any time you want until you die.

MELISSA: Help! Stop! Shaddup! Lemme outa here!

At left, A.R. Gurney as Andrew Makepeace Ladd III, with Holland Taylor as Melissa Gardner

Photo by Anita & Steve Shevett

MELISSA: Andy Ladd, is that YOU? Blow-dried and custom-tailored and jogging-trim at fifty-five? Hiding behind that lovely wife with her heels together and her hands folded discreetly over her snatch? . . . Help! Is that a *grand*child nestled in someone's arms? God, Andy, you look like the Holy Family! Season's Greetings and Happy Holidays and even Merry Christmas, Senator Ladd. We who are about to die salute you.

At right, Jane Curtin as Melissa Gardner with Edward Herrmann as Andrew Makepeace Ladd III

Photo by Anita & Steve Shevett

ANDY: Merry Christmas, old friend. How are you? Where are you these days?

MELISSA: Living in New York—alone, for a change—but the big question is, WHO am I these days? That's the toughie. I keep thinking about that strange old world we grew up in. How did it manage to produce both you and me? A stalwart upright servant of the people, and a boozed-out, cynical, lascivious old broad. The best and the worst, that's us.

At right, Elaine Stritch as Melissa Gardner with Jason Robards as Andrew Makepeace Ladd III

Photo by Anita & Steve Shevett

MELISSA

I hear you're now writing long letters twice a week to Angela Atkinson, that's what's the matter.

ANDY

O.K. Here goes. The reason I'm writing Angie Atkinson is because I just don't think I can stop writing letters, particularly to girls. As I told you before, in some ways I feel most alive when I'm holed up in some corner, writing things down. I pick up a pen, and almost immediately everything seems to take shape around me. I love to write. I love writing my parents because then I become the ideal son. I love writing essays for English, because then I am for a short while a true scholar. I love writing letters to the newspaper, notes to my friends, Christmas cards, anything where I have to put down words. I love writing you. You most of all. I always have. I feel like a true lover when I'm writing you. This letter, which I'm writing with my own hand, with my own pen, in my own penmanship, comes from me and no one else, and is a present of myself to you. It's not typewritten, though I've learned how to type. There's no copy of it, though I suppose I could use a carbon. And it's not a telephone call, which is dead as soon as it is over. No, this is just me, me the way I write, the way my writing is, the way I want to be to you, giving myself to you across a distance, not keeping or retaining any part of it for myself, giving this piece of myself to you totally, and you can tear me

37

up and throw me out, or keep me, and read me today, tomorrow, any time you want until you die.

MELISSA

Help! Stop! Shaddup! Lemme outa here!

ANDY

No, I meant what I wrote in my last letter. I've thought about it. I've thought about all those dumb things which were done to us when we were young. We had absent parents, slapping nurses, stupid rules, obsolete schooling, empty rituals, hopelessly confusing sexual customs . . . oh my God, when I think about it now, it's almost unbelievable, it's a fantasy, it's like back in the Oz books, the way we grew up. But they gave us an out in the Land of Oz. They made us write. They didn't make us write particularly well. And they didn't always give us important things to write about. But they did make us sit down, and organize our thoughts, and convey those thoughts on paper as clearly as we could to another person. Thank God for that. That saved us. Or at least saved me. So I have to keep writing letters. If I can't write them to you, I have to write them to someone else. I don't think I could ever stop writing completely. Now can I come up and see you next weekend, or better yet won't you please escape from that suburban Sing-Sing and come down here and see me? I wrote my way into this problem, and goddamn it, I'm writing my way out. I'll make another reservation at the Hotel Duncan and I promise I'll put down my pen and give you a better time.

MELISSA

Dear Andy: Guess what? Right while I was in the middle of reading your letter, Jack Duffield telephoned from Amherst and asked me for a weekend up there. So I said yes before I got to where you asked me. Sorry, sweetie, but it looks like the telephone wins in the end.

ANDY

Dear Melissa: Somehow I don't think this is the end. It could be, but I don't really think it is. At least I hope it isn't. Love, Andy.

END OF PART ONE.

(The event works best if everyone takes a short break at this point.)

PART TWO

MELISSA

Hey! Yoo-hoo! Look where I am! Florence, Ooops, I mean Firenze! I LOVE it!

ANDY

What are you doing in Florence?

MELISSA

What am I doing? I'm painting, among other things.

ANDY

Good luck on the painting. Go slow on the other things.

*   *   *

ANDY

Merry Christmas.

MELISSA

Buon Natale . . .

41

ANDY

Happy Birthday . . . Mother wrote you won an art prize in Perugia. She said it was a big deal. Congratulations . . .

MELISSA

Congratulations on making Scroll and Key, whatever that is . . .

ANDY

Merry Christmas from the Land of Oz . . .

MELISSA

Felicita Natividad from the Costa del Sol . . .

ANDY

Happy Birthday from the Sterling Library . . .

MELISSA

Hear you graduated Summa Cum Laude and with all sorts of prizes. Sounds disgusting . . .

ANDY

Anchors Aweigh! Here I am, looking like Henry Fonda in *Mister Roberts*, writing this during the midwatch on the bridge of a giant attack aircraft carrier, churning through the Mediterranean, in the wake of Odysseus and Lord Nelson and Richard Halliburton. You'll be pleased to know our guns are loaded, our planes in position, and our radar is constantly scanning the skies, all designed simply and solely to protect you against Communism. The next time you see me, I want you to salute.

MELISSA

I should have known you'd join the Navy. Now you can once again be with all boys.

ANDY

We come into La Spezia in January. Could we meet?

MELISSA

Sorry. I'll be in Zermatt in January.

ANDY

Ship will be in the Mediterranean all spring. We'll come into Naples, March 3, 4, or 5? How about standing on the pier and waving us in?

MELISSA

As French say, "Je suis desolée." Am meeting Mother in Paris in March. Why don't you sail up the Seine?

43

ANDY

Merry Christmas from Manila. I've been trans-
ferred to an Admiral's staff . . . .

MELISSA

Happy New Year from Aspen . . .

ANDY

What are you doing in Aspen?

MELISSA

Going steadily down hill.

ANDY

Hello from Hong Kong . . .

MELISSA

Goodbye to San Francisco . . .

ANDY

Konichiwa. Ohayo Gozaimas. Shore duty in Japan . . .

MELISSA

Hey, you! Rumor hath it you're hooked up with
some little Jap bar-girl out there. Say it isn't so . . .

* * *

Mother wrote that you're living with some Japanese geisha girl and your family's all upset. Is that TRUE?

* * *

Did you get my letter? You're so far away, and your Navy address is so peculiar that I'm not sure I'm reaching you. I hear you're seriously involved with a lovely Japanese lady. Would you write me about her?

ANDY

Merry Christmas and Happy New Year. I thought you might appreciate this card. It's a print by the Nineteenth Century artist Hiroshige. It's called "Two Lovers Meeting on a Bridge in the Rain." Love, Andy.

MELISSA

Hey, you sly dog! Are you getting subtle in your old age? Are you trying to TELL me something? If so, tell me MORE!

* * *

I told my psychiatrist about the great love affair you're having in Japan. I said I felt suddenly terribly jealous. He said that most American men have to get involved with a dark-skinned woman before they can connect with the gorgeous blonde goddesses they really love. He brought up James Fen-

45

nimore Cooper and Faulkner and John Ford movies and went on and on. Is that TRUE? Write me what you think. I'm dying to hear from you.

* * *

Did you get my last letter? I hope I didn't sound flip. Actually I've just become involved with someone, too. His first name is Darwin and he works on Wall Street where he believes in the survival of the fittest. I'd love to hear from you.

* * *

Your mother told my mother that you've decided to marry your Japanese friend and bring her home. Oh no! Gasp, Sob, Sigh. Say it isn't so . . .

* * *

I've decided to marry Darwin. He doesn't know it yet, but he will. Won't you at least wish me luck?

* * *

ANDY

Lieutenant Junior Grade Andrew M. Ladd, III, regrets that he is unable to accept the kind invitation of . . .

MELISSA

Dear Andy. Thank you for the lovely Japanese bowl. I'll put flowers in it when you come to visit us. *If* you come to visit us. And *if* you bring flowers. Maybe you'll just bring your Japanese war bride, and we can all sit around and discuss *Rashomon*. I know you'll like Darwin. When he laughs, it's like Pinocchio turning into a donkey. We're living in a carriage house in New Canaan close to the train station, and I've got a studio all of my own. P.S. Won't you PLEASE write me about your big romance? Mother says your parents won't even talk about it any more.

ANDY

Dear Melissa: I'm writing to tell you this. Outside of you, and I *mean* outside of you, this was probably the most important thing that ever happened to me. And I mean *was*. Because it's over, it's gone, and I'm coming home, and that's all I ever want to say about it, ever again.

* * *

MELISSA

Mr. and Mrs. Darwin H. Cobb announce the birth of their daughter Francesca . . .

ANDY

Many congratulations on the baby.

MELISSA

Harvard Law School yet! Are you getting all stuffy and self-important?

47

ANDY

As you know, I've always liked to write letters. I decided I might do better trying to write laws, which, after all, are the letters that civilization writes to itself.

MELISSA

Yes you ARE getting all stuffy and self-important. Come and have a drink with us some time. We're right on the way to New York. And sooner or later everyone comes to New York.

ANDY

Read the *New York Times* account of your show in Stamford. Sounds like you are causing a series of seismic shocks up and down the Merritt Parkway . . .

* * *

MELISSA

Don't joke about my work. There's more there than what they said in your goddamn BIBLE, the *New York Times*. Enclosed see what OTHER critics said. Notice they think I'm GOOD! I AM, too! Or could be. If I can only FOCUS . . .

ANDY

Sorry, sorry, sorry. I know you're good. I've always known it.

* * *

48

MELISSA

Hear you made Law Review, whatever that means. I assume you review laws. I wish you'd review some of the marriage laws . . .

ANDY

Just a quick note. Are you in any trouble?

MELISSA

I don't understand your last note. We're fine. All fine. Everyone's fine.

* * *

ANDY

Congratulations on baby number two . . .

MELISSA

Number two is a perfect way to describe this particular baby . . .

ANDY

Greetings from Washington. Here clerking for a Supreme Court Justice which isn't quite as fancy as it sounds . . .

* * *

MELISSA

Dear Andy: I was very sorry to hear about the death of your father. I know he was a great influence on you, and I know you loved him very much. I also know he didn't like *me*. I'm sure he thought I was bad for you, and I probably was. Still, he was a good, decent man, and I always knew where I stood with him when you'd bring me home to your family, back in the old days, back in the Land of Oz. I wish I'd had a father like that. Please accept my deepest sympathies. Love. Melissa.

ANDY

Dear Melissa. Thank you for your note on my father. I did love him. He was a classy guy, the best of his breed. Even now he's gone, I can still hear him reminding me of my obligations to my family, my country, and myself, in roughly that order. All my life, he taught me that those born to privilege have special responsibilities, which is I suppose why I came home alone from Japan, why I chose the law, and why I'll probably enter politics at some level, some time on down the line. Thanks for writing. Love. Andy.

* * *

MELISSA

Merry Christmas. I'm enclosing a snapshot mother took of me and the girls. Don't I look domestic?

50

Stop looking at my hair! By the way, you'll notice you-know-who is not in the picture.

ANDY

Thanks for the Christmas card. Are you in trouble?

MELISSA

Greetings from Reno. Could I stop by Washington on the way back East?

ANDY

Let me know when you're coming. You can meet Jane.

MELISSA

Jane?

ANDY

I'm going out with a great girl named Jane.

* * *

MELISSA

Melissa Gardner Cobb regrets that she will be unable to accept the kind invitation of . . .

ANDY

Dear Melissa: Had to add my two-cents worth to Jane's thank-you note for the wedding present.

51

(Guess who is jealously peeking over my shoulder to make sure this isn't a love letter.) First of all, thanks for the present, whatever it was. Ah, a tray! I am now told it was a tray. A *hand-painted* tray. Hand-painted by you, I'll bet. Anyway, thank you. I hope all goes well with you, as it does with us. We'll be moving to New York in the fall. I've got a job with one of those high-powered law firms. It will probably be stuffy as hell for a while, but I'll learn the ropes. Besides, it's in my home state and might be a good jumping-off place for something political a little way down the line. We BOTH want you to come to dinner once we're settled in. And don't say you never come to New York. Sooner or later everyone comes to New York, as someone once wrote me, long, long ago.

* * *

Merry Christmas from us to you. Where are you these days?

* * *

Happy Birthday. See? Even a married man never forgets.

* * *

Get well soon. Mother wrote that you had had some difficulty. I hope it's not serious, and by now you're feeling fine.

* * *

I can't remember exactly what one dozen red roses are supposed to say, but here they are, and I hope they say, "cheer up."

* * *

Hey! I sent you some flowers a while back. Did you receive them? Are you all right?

* * *

MELISSA

Dear Andy. Yes, I'm all right. Yes, I got your flowers. Yes, I'm fine. No, actually, I'm not fine, and they tell me I've got to stop running around saying I am. I'm here at this posh joint outside Boston, drying out for one hundred and fifty-five dollars a day. One of my problems is that I got slightly too dependent on the Kickapoo joy juice, a habit which they tell me I picked up during the party days back in Our Town. Another is that I slide into these terrible lows. Mummy says I drag everybody down, and I guess she's right. Aaaanyway, the result is that my Ex has taken over custody of the girls, and I'm holed up here, popping tranquilizers, talking my head off in single and group psychiatric sessions, and turning into probably the biggest bore in the greater Boston area.

ANDY

Have you thought about doing some painting again? That might help.

53

Did you get my note about taking up art? You were good, and you know it. You should keep it up.

MELISSA

I *did* get your note, I *have* taken it up, and it *helps*. Really. Thank you. I'm channeling my rage, enlarging my vision, all that. I hope all goes well with you and—wait, hold it, I'm looking it up in my little black book . . . ah hah! Jane! It's Jane. Hmmmm. I hope all's well with you and Jane.

ANDY

Merry Christmas from Andy and Jane Ladd. And Andrew the Fourth! Guess the name of the dog.

MELISSA

Porgy.

ANDY

You got it.

* * *

MELISSA

Merry Christmas from San Antonio. Am trying the Southwest. I can see the most incredible shapes from my bedroom window. And there's also a pretty incredible shape now sleeping in my bed.

ANDY

Seasons Greetings from the Ladd family. (Mother wrote you were planning to get married again.)

MELISSA

I was. I did. I'm not now.

ANDY

Donner, Rhodes and McAlister announce the appointment to partnership of Mr. Andrew M. Ladd, III . . .

MELISSA

Dear Andy: Now you're such a hot-shot lawyer, could you help me get my children back? Darwin hardly lets me near them, and when he does, they behave as if I had some contagious disease. I wasn't much of a mother, but maybe I could improve, if I just had the legal responsibility . . .

ANDY

Better stay out of this one . . . Our past connections . . . conflict of interest . . .

MELISSA

Hello from Egypt. I'm trying to start again in the cradle of civilization.

* * *

55

ANDY

Christmas Greetings from the Ladds: Andy, Jane, Drew, Nicholas, and Ted. And of course Porgy.

MELISSA

Am thinking of moving to Los Angeles. Do you know anyone in Los Angeles? Does anyone know anyone in Los Angeles?

* * *

ANDY

Joy to the World from all the Ladds. Note our new address.

MELISSA

Merry Christmas. Hey you! What's going on? Just when I decide to move to New York, I see you've scampered off to the suburbs.

ANDY

I find the suburbs generally safer.

MELISSA

Chicken.

* * *

Mother wrote that you won some important election for the Republicans. I'm terribly disap-

56

pointed. I love all politicians, but I find Democrats better in bed . . .

ANDY

I'm a liberal Republican with a strong commitment to women's rights. Doesn't that count?

MELISSA

Depends on your position.

*   *   *

MELISSA

Paintings and drawings by Melissa Gardner. The Hastings Gallery. 422 Broadway. March 18 through April 30. Opening reception March 20, 6 to 8 P.M. Note I've gone back to my *maiden* name. That's a laugh.

ANDY

Got your announcement for your new show. Good luck. P.S. I'd love to have one of your paintings. We could use a little excitement on our living room walls. Seriously. What would one cost?

MELISSA

Come to the show and find out.

ANDY

Never made your show. Sorry. Things came up.

MELISSA

Chicken again.

ANDY

You're right.

MELISSA

Actually, it's just as well. I'm going through what the critics call an "anarchistic phase." They say I'm dancing on the edge of an abyss. You'd better stay away. I might take you with me when I fall.

* * *

ANDY

Dear Friends: Jane tells me that it's about time I took a crack at the annual Christmas letter, so here goes. Let's start at the top, with our quarterback, Jane herself, who never ceases to amaze us all. Not only has she continued to be a superb mother to our three sons, but she has also managed to commute into the city and hold down a part-time job in the gift shop at the Metropolitan Museum of Art. Furthermore, she is now well on her way to completing a full-fledged master's degree in Arts Administration at SUNY Purchase. More power to Jane, so say we all.

58

We are also proud of all three boys. Young Drew was soccer captain at Exeter last fall, and hopes to go on to Yale. Nicholas, our rebel in residence, has become a computer genius in high school, and has already received several tantalizing offers for summer jobs from local electronics firms. We all know that it's tougher to place our youngsters in meaningful summer employment than to get them into Harvard, so we're very proud of how far Nick has come. Ted, our last but in no way our least, now plays the clarinet in the school band at Dickinson Country Day. Since Jane and I are barely capable of singing "You Are My Sunshine" without going disastrously flat, when we hear him produce his dulcet sounds, we look at each other "in a wild surmise".

We recently bought the family summer place from my brother and sister, and hope to spend as much time as we can there, gardening, relaxing, and as the boys say, "generally veging out". Jane and I have become killers on the tennis court, and hereby challenge all comers. If any of our friends are in the Adirondack area this summer, we expect telephone calls, we expect visits, we expect elaborate house presents.

I've enjoyed very much serving on the State Legislature. We've proposed and written a number of bills, and we've won some and lost some. All my life I've had the wish to do something in the way of public service, and it has been a great pleasure to put that wish into practice. For those of my friends who have urged me to seek higher office, let me simply say that I have more than enough challenges right here where I am.

Jane and the boys join me in wishing each and all of you a Happy Holiday Season.

MELISSA

Dear Andy. If I ever get another one of those drippy Xeroxed Christmas letters from you, I think I'll invite myself out to your ducky little house for dinner, and when you're all sitting there eating terribly healthy food and discussing terribly important things and generally congratulating yourselves on all your accomplishments, I think I'll stand up on my chair, and turn around, and moon the whole fucking family!

ANDY

You're right. It was a smug dumb letter and I apologize for it. Jane normally writes it, and it sounds better when she does. I always felt better writing to just one person at a time, such as to you. I guess what I was really saying is that as far as my family is concerned, we're all managing to hold our heads above water in this tricky world. Jane and I have had our problems, but we're comfortable with each other now, and the boys, for the moment, are out of trouble. Nicky seems to be off drugs now, and Ted is getting help on his stammer. Porgy, Jr., my old cocker, died, and I miss him too much to get a replacement. I'm thinking of running for the Senate next fall if O'Hara retires. What do you think? I'd really like your opinion. If you decide to answer this, you might write care of my office address. Jane has a slight tendency toward melo-

60

drama, particularly after she got ahold of your last little note.

MELISSA

The Senate yet! I should have known. Oh Andy, just think! Once again, you can be with all boys. Oh hell, go for it, if you want. You'll be an image of righteousness and rectitude in our god-forsaken land. Or maybe it's just me that's godforsaken these days.

* * *

ANDY

The Honorable Andrew M. Ladd III wishes to express his thanks for your generous donation to his senatorial campaign . . . You sent too MUCH, Melissa! You didn't need to.

* * *

MELISSA

Greetings from Silver Hill. Slight regression in the liquor department. They say it's in the genes. Lord knows, my mother has the problem, and my father, too, in the end. Anyway, I'm working on it. Darwin is being a real shit about the girls. He's cut down on my visitation rights, so when you get to Washington, I want you to write a special law about vindictive ex-husbands, banishing them to Lower Slobbovia, forever and ever. Amen.

61

ANDY

Seasons Greetings from Senator and Mrs. Andrew
M. Ladd and family.

MELISSA

Season's Greetings indeed! Is that all you can say to
me after forty years? I'm warning you, Andy. Keep
that shit up, and I swear I'll come down and moon
the whole Senate.

ANDY

Sorry. My staff sent that out. Merry Christmas, old
friend. How are you? Where are you these days?

MELISSA

Living in New York—alone, for a change—but the
big question is, WHO am I these days? That's the
toughie. I keep thinking about that strange old
world we grew up in. How did it manage to produce both you and me? A stalwart upright servant
of the people, and a boozed out, cynical, lascivious
old broad. The best and the worst, that's us.

ANDY

Don't be so tough on yourself. Get back to your art.

62

MELISSA

I'll try.

* * *

ANDY

Merry Christmas, Happy New Year, and much love.

MELISSA

Much LOVE? MUCH love? God, Andy, how sexy! Remember how much that meant in our preppy days? If it was just "love" you were out in the cold, and if it was "all my love," you were hemmed in for life—but "Much Love" meant that things could go either way. Remember?

* * *

ANDY

Merry Christmas and love from us all.

MELISSA

Saw you on *Sixty Minutes*. You looked fabulous. And that was a great little pep talk in the Senate on "our responsibilities" to Latin America. But don't forget to keep your eye on the ball.

63

ANDY

Thanks for your card. What ball?

MELISSA

The ball is that money doesn't solve everything. It helps, but not as much as people think. Take it from one who knows. That's the ball.

* * *

ANDY

Merry Christmas and love. What are you up to these days?

MELISSA

I'm trying to work with clay. Remember that kind of clay we used in Mrs. Mickler's art class in fourth grade? That old gray stuff? We called it plasticene. I'm trying to work with that. I'm making cats, dogs . . . I even made a kangaroo jumping over a glass of orange juice. Remember that? I'm trying to get back to some of those old, old feelings I had back in the Homeland. I have to find feelings, any feelings, otherwise I'm dead. Come down and help me search. I have a studio down in Soho and we could . . . um, er, uh, well we could at least have DIN-NER and talk about old times, couldn't we, Senator Ladd? P.S. Did you know that my mother got married again? At the age of eighty-two? To my father's BROTHER yet! So now you have to call her Mrs. Gardner again, just like the old days. The wheel seems to be coming around full circle. Hint, hint.

ANDY

A quick note on the way to the airport. When you write, put "attention Mrs. Walpole" on the envelope. She's my private secretary, I've alerted her, and she'll pass your letters directly on to me. Otherwise, the whole office staff seems to get a peek. In haste . . .

MELISSA

I'm having a show opening January 28 through Feb 25. Won't you come? I'd love to have you see what I've been up to. Maybe it will ring a few old bells.

ANDY

Can't make it. I'll be on an official visit to the Philippines most of February, then a week's spring skiing at Stowe with the boys. Good luck.

*   *   *

How did the show go?

*   *   *

Haven't heard from you. Tell me about the show.

*   *   *

65

I want to hear from you. Please.

MELISSA

The show stank. The crowd hated it, the critics
hated it, I hated it. It was nostalgic shit. You can't
go home again, and you can quote me on that. I'm
turning to photography now. Realism! That's my
bag. The present tense. Look at the modern world
squarely in the face, and don't blink . . . Oh
Andy, couldn't I see you? You're all I have left.

ANDY

I'll be in New York next Tuesday the 19th. Have to
make a fund-raising speech at a dinner. I could
stop by your place afterwards.

MELISSA

I'll be there all evening.

* * *

ANDY

Red roses. This time I think I know what they
mean.

MELISSA

All I know is that after last night I want to see you
again.

* * *

66

Any chance of any other fund-raisers coming up in
the near future?

* * *

Mrs. Walpole, are you there? Are you delivering
the mail?

* * *

ANDY

I'm sorry I've taken so long to reply. I've been
upstate mending a few fences, and then to Zurich
for a three-day economic conference, and then a
weekend with Jane, mending a few fences *there*
. . . Darling, I'll have to ask you not to telephone
the office. Every call has to be logged in, and most
of them get screened by these over-eager college
interns who like to rush back to Cambridge and
New Haven and announce to their classmates in
political science that Senator Ladd is shacking up
on the side. The phones simply aren't secure. At
long last, the letter beats out the telephone, my
love! And guess what? I'm writing this with the old
Parker 51 my grandmother gave when I went
away to school. I found it in the back of my bureau
drawer with my Scroll and Key pin, and my Lieutenant J.G. bars from the Navy, and the Zippo
lighter you gave me at some dance. The pen didn't
even work at first. I had to clean it out, and then
traipse all over Washington looking for a store
which still sells a bottle of ink. Anyway, it feels
good holding this thing again. It feels good writing

to you again. Longhand. Forming my d's and t's the way Miss Emerson taught us so long ago. I know you've never liked writing letters, but now you HAVE to! Ha, ha. As for business: I plan to come through New York next Wednesday, and I'll call you from the airport if there's time to stop by.

MELISSA

Sweetheart, I LOVED seeing you. Come again . . .

ANDY

. . . will be stopping through a week from next . . .

MELISSA

. . . Did you ever *dream* we'd be so good at sex?

ANDY

. . . . Two up-tight old Wasps going at it like a sale at Brooks Brothers . . .

MELISSA

. . . I figure fifty years went into last night . . .

ANDY

. . . . Let's go for a hundred . . . .

MELISSA

. . . Oh my God, come again soon, or sooner . . .

ANDY

. . . I'm already making plans . . .

MELISSA

. . . have to go to San Francisco to visit the girls. Couldn't we meet somewhere on the way?

ANDY

. . . I don't see how we can possibly go public . . .

MELISSA

. . . some country inn, some deliciously seedy motel . . .

ANDY

. . . I don't see how . . .

MELISSA

. . . see you more than for just a few hours . . .

ANDY

. . . price we have to pay . . .

69

MELISSA

. . . I'm getting so I think about nothing but how
we can . . .

ANDY

. . . I'm not sure I can change my whole life so
radically . . .

MELISSA

. . . other politicians have gotten divorced . . .
Rockefeller, Reagan . . .

ANDY

. . . Jane . . . the children . . . my particular
constituency . . .

MELISSA

. . . you've become the center of my life. If you
left, I don't think I could . . .

ANDY

. . . because of the coming election, I don't see
how we can . . .

MELISSA

Dear Andy: A reporter called up from the Daily
News. What do I do about it?

70

ANDY

Nothing.

MELISSA

I suppose you know all this, but there's a crack about us in Newsweek. And Mother heard some radio talk show where they actually named names. What should I do? Go away? What?

ANDY

Nothing.

MELISSA

They called Darwin, you know. They tracked him down. The son of a bitch told them this has been going on for years.

ANDY

Wish it had been.

MELISSA

Now they're telephoning. What do I say?

ANDY

Say we're good old friends.

71

MELISSA

Friends, I like. Good, I like. Old, I'm beginning to
have problems with.

ANDY

Then don't say anything. Hang up. This, too, shall
pass.

MELISSA

Will I be seeing you again?

ANDY

Better not, for a while.

MELISSA

I meant, after the election . . .

ANDY

Better lie low for a while.

MELISSA

I miss you terribly . . .

ANDY

Better lie low.

72

MELISSA

I NEED you, Andy. You're my anchor man these days. Without you, I'm not sure I can . . .

ANDY

Hold on now. Just hold on . . .

MELISSA

. . . where were you? I waited three hours hoping that you'd at least call . . .

ANDY

. . . please don't telephone . . . Mrs. Walpole was sick that day and . . .

MELISSA

. . . I haven't seen you in over a month now . . .

ANDY

. . . the coming election . . .

MELISSA

. . . surely you could at least take time out to . . .

ANDY

. . . if I want to be reelected . . .

73

MELISSA

. . . I need you. I need to be with you. I don't know if I can . . .

ANDY

. . . the election . . . the election . . . the election . . .

* * *

MELISSA

I haven't heard from you in six weeks, Andy.

* * *

Are you trying to tell me something, Andy?

* * *

Is this it, Andy?

* * *

Congratulations on landslide victory. Love. Melissa.

ANDY

Could we meet at your place next Sunday night?

74

MELISSA

Oh thank God . . .

ANDY

I meant that we have to talk, Melissa . . .

MELISSA

Uh oh. Talk. I'm scared of talk. In fact, I dread
it . . .

* * *

ANDY

Dearest Melissa: Are you all right? That was a
heavy scene last Sunday, but I know I'm right.
We've got to go one way or the other, and the
other leads nowhere. I know I sound like a stuffy
prick, but I do feel I have a responsibility to Jane,
and the boys, and now, after the election, to my
constituency, which had enough faith and trust in
me to vote me back in despite all that crap in the
newspapers. And it wouldn't work with us anyway,
in the long run, sweetheart. We're too old. We're
carrying too much old baggage on our backs. We'd
last about a week if we got married. But we can
still write letters, darling. We can always do that.
Letters are still our strength and our salvation.
Mrs. Walpole is still with us, and there's no reason
why we can't continue to keep in touch with each
other in this wonderful old way. I count on your

75

letters, darling. I always have. And I hope you will count on mine . . .

* * *

Are you there? I keep putting "please forward" on the envelopes but who knows . . .

* * *

Now I've even resorted to the telephone, but all I get is your damn machine . . . Please. I need to hear from you . . .

* * *

Senator and Mrs. Andrew M. Ladd, III, and family send you warm Holiday greetings and every good wish for the New Year.

MELISSA

Andy Ladd, is that YOU? Blow dried and custom-tailored and jogging-trim at fifty-five. Hiding behind that lovely wife with her heels together and her hands folded discreetly over her snatch? And is that your new DOG, Andy? I see you've graduated to a Golden Retriever. And are those your sons and heirs? And—Help!—is that a *grand*child nestled in someone's arms? God, Andy, you look like the Holy Family! Season's Greetings and Happy Holidays and even Merry Christmas, Senator Ladd. We who are about to die salute you . . .

76

ANDY

Just reread your last note. What's this "we who are about to die" stuff?

* * *

May I see you again?

* * *

I want to see you again, if I may.

* * *

Dear Mrs. Gardner. I seem to have lost touch with Melissa again. I wonder if you might send me her latest address.

* * *

Dear Melissa. Your mother wrote that you'd returned to the Land of Oz. I'm flying up next Thursday to see you.

MELISSA

No! Please! Don't! Please stay away! I've let myself go. I'm fat, I'm ugly, my hair is horrible! I'm locked in at the funny farm all week, and then Mother gets me weekends if I'm good. They've put me on all sorts of new drugs, and half the time I don't make sense at all! I can't even do finger-painting now without fucking it up. My girls won't even

77

talk to me on the telephone now. They say I upset them too much. Oh, I've made a mess of things, Andy. I've made a total, ghastly mess. I don't like life any more. I hate it. Sometimes I think that if you and I had just . . . if we had just . . . oh but just stay away, Andy. Please.

ANDY

Arriving Saturday morning. Will meet you at your mother's.

MELISSA

DON'T! I don't want to see you! I won't be there! I'll be GONE, Andy! I swear. I'll be gone.

* * *

ANDY

Dear Mrs. Gardner: I think the first letter I ever wrote was to you, accepting an invitation for Melissa's birthday party. Now I'm writing you again about her death. I want to say a few things on paper I couldn't say at her funeral, both when I spoke, and when you and I talked afterward. As you may know, Melissa and I managed to keep in touch with each other most of our lives, primarily through letters. Even now, as I write this letter to you, I feel I'm writing it also to her.

MELISSA

Ah, you're in your element now, Andy . . .

78

ANDY

We had a complicated relationship, she and I, all
our lives. We went in very different directions. But
somehow over all those years, I think we managed
to give something to each other. Melissa expressed
all the dangerous and rebellious feelings I never
dared admit to . . .

MELISSA

Now he tells me . . .

ANDY

And I like to think I gave her some sense of balance . . .

MELISSA

BALANCE? Oh Hell, I give up. Have it your way,
Andy: balance.

ANDY

Most of the things I did in life I did with her partly
in mind. And if I said or did an inauthentic thing, I
could almost hear her groaning over my shoulder.
But now she's gone I really don't know how I'll get
along without her.

MELISSA

(Looking at him for the first time.) You'll survive,
Andy . . .

79

ANDY

I have a wonderful wife, fine children, and a place in the world I feel proud of, but the death of Melissa suddenly leaves a huge gap in my life . . .

MELISSA

Oh now, Andy . . .

ANDY

The thought of never again being able to write to her, to connect to her, to get some signal back from her, fills me with an emptiness which is hard to describe.

MELISSA

Now Andy, stop . . .

ANDY

I don't think there are many men in this world who have had the benefit of such a friendship with such a woman. But it was more than friendship, too. I know now that I loved her. I loved her even from the day I met her, when she walked into second grade, looking like the lost princess of Oz.

MELISSA

Oh, Andy, PLEASE. I can't bear it.

80

ANDY

I don't think I've ever loved anyone the way I loved her, and I know I never will again. She was at the heart of my life, and already I miss her desperately. I just wanted to say this to you and to her. Sincerely, Andy Ladd.

MELISSA

Thank you, Andy.

THE END.